Little Michael's Quiz For Parents
Circle True or False

1. I love my kids no matter what.   T   F

2. I hug my kids a lot.   T   F

3. I'm patient with my kids.   T   F

4. I read about raising good kids.   T   F

5. I'm proud when my kids act like me.   T   F

6. I can make a paper airplane.   T   F

If you got any false answers I think my book will help you a lot. Even how to make planes!

My Guarantee

If you don't like my book. Just tell me. I'll give you back all your money. Please keep my book anyway. Give it to someone else who might like it better.

Your friend,
Little Michael

Little Michael's Guide To Raising Good Parents
A Seven Year Old's View

Michael Joseph Riso

Continuous Learning Publishers
Buffalo, New York

ISBN 0-9668103-0-9

LCCN 98-93806

Printed in the United States

SPAN
Small Publishers Association
of North America

This book is dedicated to my parents Frank and Mary Lou who taught me wonderful values and encouraged me to think for myself.

"To see people as they really are we must love them unconditionally. Unless we do so, they may not reveal themselves to us and we will miss them forever."

Leo Buscaglia

Acknowledgements

Thank you to my young nephew Shane Biggs for his penmanship during the early stages of the book's development, and my nephew Frankie Wright for his early sketches.

Thank you to Jimmie Gilliam who took me under her wing and offered her valuable guidance on how to excel as a writer.

Thank you to Bob Aradio for his cover design and character illustrations. Without Bob's creative abilities, this book could not have fully expressed my deepest heartfelt emotions.

Thank you to my mom and editor for making sure I punctuated everything correctly and that I didn't allow my sentences to run on.

Thank you to Jeannie. You have taught me much about myself. Most importantly, how to love unconditionally.

Thank you to Jenni Aradio for her graphic expertise and late night snacks, and baby Kayla Mariin for reminding us what it's like to be a child.

Thank you to Nancy Parisi for her ability to photograph me in a relaxed, natural manner.

Thank you to my family, friends, and antagonists, all who helped me become who I am.

Thank you to the imaginative young students from St. Margaret's, St. Mark, St. Rose of Lima, St. Peter and Paul, and Hillview Elementary for their finger paintings and creative stories.

Table of contents

About the Author

About the Illustrator

Foreword

Preface

A letter from Little Michael

Chapters   page

Foreword

Do you remember the first time you held your child? Do you recall the hopes and dreams you had and how you would provide everything for your child you wished you had received when you were growing up? Did you remember these fond thoughts the first time your child kept you up all night?

We tend to complicate things as adults and lose track of how simple and clear our children's needs are. Little Michael speaks to the parent in all of us and tells us in very straightforward terms what he and his fellow children need from us and what makes life harder for them.

If this book makes you sad, tell your child that you are sorry and that it is sometimes hard to be a good parent. If it makes you angry, you may need to figure out what nerve it strikes. If it makes you happy and you do well on the quizzes, thank your parents for being a good example.

Joseph G. Langen, Ph.D.
Licensed psychologist and family therapist

Here's What People Are Saying About
Little Michael's Guide To Raising Good Parents:

I read Little Michael's Guide two days ago. Today, I took the day off work and spent it with my children. We made applesauce and raked leaves. It took twice as long doing it with them in mind, however what a wonderful day we all had. I sometimes allow life to get me sidetracked. Little Michael was an endearing reminder of the parenting I expect of myself.

Jackie Mordaunt
Grand Island, NY

Mike's book is excellent! Once I started reading it, I couldn't put it down. I wish I had been able to read it years ago when I was raising my kids.

Alice Allan
Tonawanda, NY

As a parent this book not only opened my eyes, it opened my heart.

John Kiebzak
Largo, FL

Little Michael is enlightening even if you don't have children. It's worth every cent, solely for the memories it brings to mind.

Bonnie Morgan
Getzville, NY

A must read for everyone. Thoroughly enjoyable.

David Bennett
Chagrin Falls, OH

Preface

I grew up in Buffalo, New York in a very loving family. My mom and dad, Mary Lou and Frank, did a wonderful job instilling good values in all seven children. Among them thinking for ourselves, not necessarily following the crowd. This came in handy when it came to decisions concerning friendships, smoking, drinking, honesty, making fun of others, and choosing if and when to have sex. Looking back, much of what we learned was from watching mom and dad's behavior around us and their interactions with adults and their children. I'm proud they were such great role models. This book is for everyone who could benefit by receiving direction on how to positively influence their children by their own behavior. There is not another job more vital than the influence we impart on the young.

Little Michael's Guide To Raising Good Parents wasn't a book I planned to write. It happened as I was writing one afternoon at a local restaurant. I glanced up at the bar as people drank, smoked, and conversed, and wondered what type of parents they might be, and what a young child might think. Before the day was over, the first draft of the book was complete.

When we were young children we instinctively knew what we wanted from our parents. However, once we became adults our memories seemed to fade. Our kids want the same things we did as youngsters-time with us, positive direction, and love. I hope you gain as much insight into children as I did while thinking like little seven year old Michael.

Michael Joseph Riso

Buffalo, 1998

Hi, I'm Little Michael. I'm seven years old. I know parents want to get along with us kids better. But, they don't always have such an easy job. I'm not a psychologist. But, I think I can help grown ups understand us little kids better. So, I wrote a book to help you get some ideas on what we really want from you. It's only my first book. So, I hope you like it.

P.S. My mom helped me look up psychologist in the dictionary.

Little Michael
Age 7

1. You were a kid

Sometimes I think you forgot what it's like to be a little kid. I know you know because I saw pictures when you were little. You rode your bike, went to see movies, went swimming and played in the yard. You were happy with your friends. It was a lot of fun, remember?

Mom age 4

You were a kid

2. I'm curious

Since I was little I wanted to know about things I didn't know, so I asked. A lot of times no one wants to answer. The other day my dad told me to stop asking so many questions. How am I supposed to learn things I don't know? I just turned seven.

I'm curious

3. I'm not dad

Sometimes you make me feel like I'm supposed to act like dad. Mom keeps saying study hard Michael and some day you can be a doctor just like dad and grandpa Carl. I don't want to be a doctor. I'm going to be a deep sea diver or a cowboy.

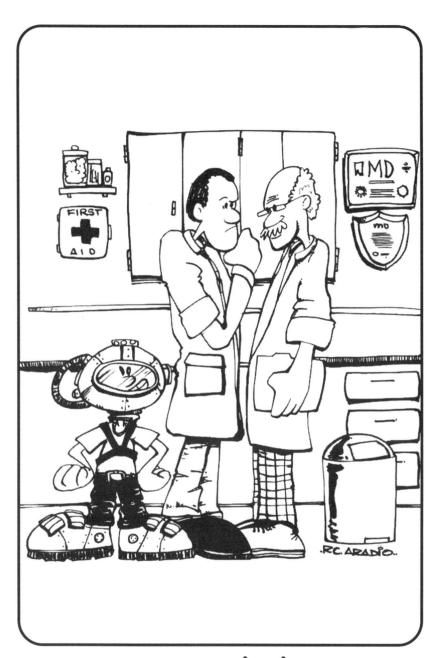

I'm not dad

4. Stop yelling at me

I don't like being yelled at. It hurts my feelings and makes me want to cry even though I don't. Yesterday I got dirty playing tag. Mom didn't even get mad. I got dirty today and she yelled at me. Is playing tag and getting dirty okay?

Stop yelling at me

5. I want some rules

When my mom and dad say okay to everything I ask for, I think they don't care what I do. Sometimes I do things I don't really want to so they notice me. Like bringing worms into the house. Lots of times I act mad when they say no. But I'm mostly pretending.

I want some rules

6. Look at me

I tried to tell dad about my gold star in school. Lots of times when I'm talking he doesn't look. He's too busy watching TV or reading the paper, or working on his computer. How do I tell if he's listening to me? Mostly he doesn't anyway. He's always too busy.

Look at me

7. You shouldn't lie

I know lying is wrong. You told me so about a million times. I don't like having to stay in my room when I lie. Then how come you can lie mom? You said to that man on the phone we have a whole set of encyclopedias and we don't. I think you should have to stay in your room for a day. No, a whole week!

You shouldn't lie

8. TV isn't the same as you

I really like watching all the fun shows on TV. I can't stop playing my video games because I'm really good. I beat most all my friends. I liked going to the aquarium last week with mom, dad, Alison and my cat Zeek even better than watching TV. Playing baseball with dad and flying my airplane with mom was more fun too. I wish we did more things together.

TV isn't the same as you

9. I Know all about sex

I learned everything from my eight year old friend Alex. He told me not to hold any girl's hand because she might get pregnant. I won't. If I did then I'd have to marry her. I can't. I'm too little! Mom and dad must have held hands. That's how come I'm here.

I know all about sex

10. Take a vacation

Mom and dad act like I'm a bother some days. I even make mom cry when I'm bad. They need to go away and be alone. I saw some pretty pictures. Florida and Hawaii look nice. I promise I'd be good when they're gone. But they would have to promise scouts honor to come back. Because I'll miss them a lot.

Take a vacation

Connect the dots for my secret message

Draw lines between the dots

A   1-13

B   1-7, 1-9, & 1-7

C   1-9

D   1-3 & 1-5

23

11. I'm only seven

Mom says I should know better.
 How? I'm only seven.
She says why don't you act like
your big brother?
I can't I'm only seven.
She says Michael act your age.
I am mom,

I'm seven!

I'm only seven

12. Because I said so

Mom, turn off the television.

Why, Michael?

Because I said so.

Michael, can't I finish watching?

It's the Academy Awards.

Not tonight honey.

Why?

Because I said so.

But there's only ten minutes left.

Mom, I said shut it off now, or you're going right to your room.

But why can't I watch, Michael?

Because I'm your son, and I said so.

Because I said so

13. Let me make some mistakes

Michael let me do that for you. I'll help you put that toy together Mikey.

Here Mikey, let me show you the right way.

I wish mom and dad would let me try some things by myself. I can learn on my own. Anyway, I'd tell them if it got too hard to do.

Let me make some mistakes

14. I could use some help

My friends were drinking beer. Max got it from his dad's fridge. I tried a little. It tasted rotten and I felt funny after. Then we went to the store. We stole snickers bars. I only took a little one, so I know it wasn't that bad. My friend Paul took a real big one. I think he might get in trouble if someone finds out. I'm pretty sure I won't because mine was so small. Joey Turk was kissing Mary Martin. Yuck! I hope he didn't hold her hand.

I could use some help

15. Stop Promising

We'll go golfing as soon as I get a free day Michael.

Maybe we'll go to the baseball game tomorrow Son.

Sorry Mikey, I've got some work to catch up on. We'll play cards another time.

I get mad when mom and dad keep saying things they never do. I wish they just wouldn't say anything at all.

Stop Promising

16. Don't argue when I'm home

I don't know why mom and dad yell at each other. Don't they like each other? I wish they would tell me before they're going to yell, so I can run to my room. Yelling scares me. Even if I don't get yelled at. Sometimes I see mom cry after dad leaves. And I give her a hug. Then I feel very sad.

Don't argue when I'm home

17. I notice

The kids play basketball, baseball, and street hockey and so do I. Dad yells a lot on the phone with his business and doesn't always pick up his clothes. How come I have to? Sometimes mom talks on the phone about people she doesn't like. I heard her say she was glad grandma Peterson wasn't her mom. I bet grandma's feelings would be hurt if I told her. But, I wouldn't tell her because I love her.

I notice

18. I do what you do

I tried my first cigarette. It made me cough and choke. Mom and dad must smoke better ones. Mom, dad and their friends drink almost every day. It makes them laugh. I like laughing. Maybe I'll try that too. Mom pretended she was sick from work yesterday. I'll pretend to be sick next week. I'm good at acting. Then I can stay home from school. It must be okay to lie about being sick when you don't want to go some place.

I do what you do

39

Little Michael's list of all time best candy and snacks

Flying saucers

Bazooka gum

Tootsie rolls

Pez candy

Licorice rope

Sno caps

Raisinets

Goobers

Jawbreakers

Rootbeer barrels

Ho Ho's

Twinkies

Bundt cake

Rice Krispie treats

Homemade cookies

Bugles

Fritos corn chips

Neapolitan ice cream

Cheetos

Jello

Add your favorites

_____

_____

_____

Hot tamales	Brownies
Hershey's kisses	Oreos
M&M's	Whoppers
Fireballs	Lifesavers
Ju Ju Bees	Smarties
Pixy Stix	Candy buttons
Pop tarts	Pudding
Ginger snaps	Fig Newtons
Starburst	Juicyfruit
Snickers	3 Musketeers
Milky Way	Reese's peanut butter cups
Baby Ruth	Butterfinger
Chocolate babies	Boston baked beans
Lemonheads	Mike and Ike
Dots	Good & Plenty
Red hot dollars	Butterfinger

19. Say you're sorry

Mom, I know you don't always mean to get mad at me. And sometimes I'm bad and I know it. That's why you yell. When you're real mad you cry. I hug you and say I'm sorry for being bad. I feel better then. Maybe you could say you're sorry to me too. Then you'd feel better like me.

Say you're Sorry

20. I'm only a kid once

When I get to be grown up I'll
do grown up things. I'll probably get
a job, cut the grass, and drive a
car. Right now I'm still a little kid.
And I want to ride my bike.
Play football with my friends
and catch salamanders.

I'm only a kid once

21. I finally did it

I filled my whole stamp book. 54 different stamps. The last was the hardest. Tanzania. I'm not sure where that is. Mom knows where a map is. I'll ask her. I told her about getting the last stamp from grandpa. She hugged me and kissed my head. She was very proud of me. She gave me $5. Wow! And said I could go buy another stamp album. I thought I already had all the stamps in the world!

I finally did it

22. You can't hug me too much

I pretend I don't want you to hug me because my friends think it isn't cool. I like being hugged by mom and dad and from my big sister Alison even though I pretend sometimes I don't. It's okay at grandma's. And at my house before bed. After my friends go home.

You can't hug me too much

23. I want to be like zeek

My pet cat zeek likes when I play with him. I do it a lot. He can't talk. I know he likes it because he just lies there and purrs. Meow. Meow. Meow.
I wish I could be like zeek so mom and dad would play with me more. I'm serious! Reading to me would be awesome too.
zeek likes that too.

I want to be like zeek

24. I really want you

We have two cars, a big house with a garden, a boat, three TV's, two stereos and CD, a blue pool, and lots of expensive stuff. Mom and dad tell their friends about them all the time. I just won best drawing in my school class. It was of a happy family. Dad hasn't hugged me lately and mom's not home much. Mom shops a lot and dad works late a lot. Buying lots of things must make them happier than my best drawing ever.

I really want you

25. Everyone needs love

My friend Gary has a turtle. I got to rub his shell. I think he liked it. I'm pretty sure he's a boy not a girl because he's so strong. We found a gigantic caterpillar on the tree that was green, yellow, red, orange, and black. He walked along. We picked him up. And we petted him very carefully. We saw him smile. But nobody believes he did. But he really did! My friend Kathy's mom had to go to the hospital. Kathy was very sad and cried. I hugged her so she wouldn't be scared and then she felt better.

Everyone needs love

26. Little Michael's Rules For Being A Good Parent

1. Tell us you love us. Show us you love us.
2. Hug us a lot.
3. Act like you want us to act.
4. Remember our age. We're still learning. Be patient.
5. Talk to us and don't yell.
6. Tell the truth.
7. Do what you say or don't say it.
8. Let us have fun being kids.
9. Read books to learn about us kids.
10. Be happy inside. You'll be happy outside.

Cut this out to Help!

26. Little Michael's Rules For Being A Good Parent

1. Tell us you love us. Show us you love us.
2. Hug us a lot.
3. Act like you want us to act.
4. Remember our age. We're still learning. Be patient.
5. Talk to us and don't yell.
6. Tell the truth.
7. Do what you say or don't say it.
8. Let us have fun being kids.
9. Read books to learn about us kids.
10. Be happy inside. You'll be happy outside.

27. My Rules When You're Grounded

1. No driving the car.
2. No TV at all.
3. No friends can come over.
4. No going to friends.
5. Go to your room after dinner.
6. No cigarettes <u>forever!</u>
7. No drinking alcohol.
8. No reading the paper.
9. No talking on the phone.
   (in the car either!)
10. No playing with Zeek.

Remember your rules!

26. Little Michael's Rules For Being A Good Parent

1. Tell us you love us. Show us you love us.
2. Hug us a lot.
3. Act like you want us to act.
4. Remember our age. We're still learning. Be patient.
5. Talk to us and don't yell.
6. Tell the truth.
7. Do what you say or don't say it.
8. Let us have fun being kids.
9. Read books to learn about us kids.
10. Be happy inside. You'll be happy outside.

28. Please answer true or false
(Be real honest)

1. I love all my kids.   T   F
2. I liked being a little kid.   T   F
3. I hug my kids a lot.   T   F
4. I'm glad when my
   kids act like me.   T   F
5. I like getting yelled at.   T   F
6. I want a vacation.   T   F
7. I'm patient with my kids.   T   F
8. I watch TV too much.   T   F
9. I don't ever lie.   T   F
10. I never make mistakes.
    Only everyone else does.   T   F
11. I don't need help ever.   T   F

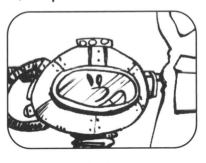

12. I let my kids have fun.   T   F

13. I read about raising good kids.   T   F

14. I'm friendlier to the pet than
    my kids.   T   F

15. I'm a really happy person.   T   F

16. I love my kids no matter what.   T   F

Numbers 1,2,3,4,6,7,9,12,13,15, and 16 should be true.

Numbers 5,8,10,11, and 14 should be false.

P.S. Its okay if sometimes you answered sometimes.

I hope you did a good score!

29. Your homework

Write your answers on the lines.

Write 3 things that make you happiest.

1. _____

2. _____

3. _____

Write 3 things you liked when you were little.

1. _____

2. _____

3. _____

How do you like it when you get yelled at?

_____

_____

What's the last time you lied.* Even if you didn't mean to.

_____

*Don't do it again!

Write 3 places you can go on vacation.

1. _____

2. _____

3. _____

Draw you having fun when you were little in the boxes. It's okay if you can't draw good.

Put down 3 mistakes* you wish you could take back because they made you feel bad.

1. _____

2. _____

3. _____

*I forgive you.

Put down 1 thing you promise to do with your kids (no lying).

1. _____

When the kids are home I promise to:
 (circle one)

not argue   not argue   not argue

If you were little which would you pick? Choose one. (circle it)

jump rope   go to work

clean the house   go to grandma's

ride my bike   have mom read to me

Things you can do to feel better when you're sad.

Pet a baby kitten.

Pet a tiny puppy.

Let a puppy lick your face.

Run and splash in rain puddles.

Tell someone you're sorry.

Watch the wizard of oz.

Hug a kid. A grown up is okay too.

Find some pretty leaves to collect.

Say I love you to someone you know
you should. Don't even wait one
second! Mark an (x) when you've
told them.

my dad( )   my brother( )

my mom( )   my sister( )

my grandma( )   my grandpa( )

my daughter( )   my son( )

my cat Zeek( )   my friend( )

* Homework has to be handed in tomorrow.

65

30. Stories From Little Kids That Will Make You Smile

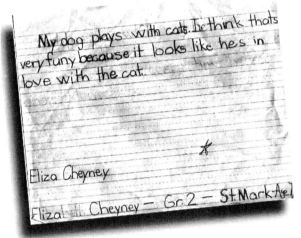

My dog plays with cats. I think thats very funy because it looks like he's in love with the cat.

Eliza Cheyney

Elizah Cheyney — Gr.2 — StMark Ag.7

Eliza Cheyney
Age 7
Grade 2
St. Mark

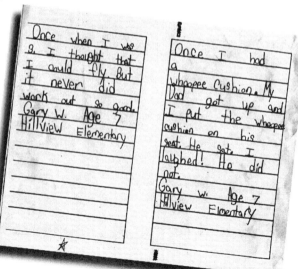

Gary westberg
Age 7
Grade 2
Hillview Elementary

Once when I was 8. I thought that I could fly. But it never did work out so good.
Gary W. Age 7
Hillview Elementary

Once I had a whoopee cushion. My Dad got up and I put the whoopee cushion on his seat. He sat. I laughed! He did not.
Gary W. Age 7
Hillview Elementary

Pumpkin's are funny because on halloween the faces look like they will make the pumpkin grow arms and legs and go out scareing people. Clown's are funny because they make funny faces and hit them selfs on the head with bats.

Emily Shatzel - Gr.2 - St.Mark-Age7

Emily Shatzel
Age 7
Grade 2
St. Mark

Anthony Phommachanh
Age 6
Grade 2
St. Margaret's

One day my mom was changing my brother. Sometimes my mom gives him air, she keeps his diper off. My dad was playing with my brother and my brother peed on my dad.
Anthony Phommachanh
St. Margaret school
age 6

Katie Hatmilton 7 years old.
S.s. peter and Paul williamsville, NY
Once upon a time a scarecrow went to the zoo. He scared all the animals away. The zoo kepper ran away too.

Katie Hamilton
Age 6
Grade 2
St. Peter and Paul

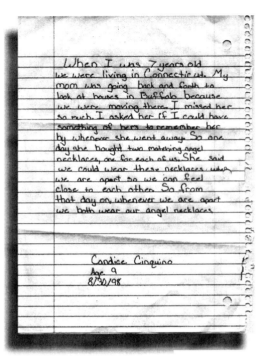

When I was 7 years old we were living in Connecticut. My mom was going back and forth to look at houses in Buffalo because we were moving there. I missed her so much. I asked her if I could have something of hers to remember her by whenever she went away. So one day she bought two matching angel necklaces, one for each of us. She said we could wear these necklaces when we are apart so we can feel close to each other. So from that day on, whenever we are apart we both wear our angel necklaces.

Candice Cinquino
Age 9
8/30/98

Candice Cinquino
Age 9

Peter Pantano
Age 7
Grade 2
St. Margaret's

Peter

It was Gim to day. evreay one was chaging for Gim. they came out from chaing Mad Millans. fraadt his pans. he was in birst. he sceamed lod. he was so in birst. he ran home. in poublike. he staed home all week he was so nuts.

R.J. Surowick
Age 7
Grade 2
Hillview
Elementary

My birthday was very funny. I got a Barbie doll. I'm a boy!

R.J.   Age 7
Hillview Elementary

---

7 years old Gabriella Petrelli   SS. Peter and Paul winners

Once apoun a time there was a dinosoar and it almost ate his tail and his mom and his dad and one day he was playing with his friend a he was playing tag well he wast really playing tag he was trying to eat his friend! and when his mom and dad calld him in he charged at his mom and dad and bumed his head on a trysarotops and that trysarotops got crasy and he was punching his head!

Gabriella Petrelli
Age 7
Grade 2
St. Peter and Paul

69

31. Finger Painting with My Friends

I thought you would like to see how good my friends are at finger paints. But I couldn't fit everyone, but here are some really good ones. Over 200 students helped with their drawings. They're for sale for 5 cents each if you like them. I better ask my mom first if it's okay because maybe 5 cents is too much. If you buy one I promise I'll give the money to the one who painted it.

Little Michael

> "I did it because it was fun,
>   and fun is good."
>   Dr. Seuss

Bethany Cleveland Age 5
Hillview Elementary

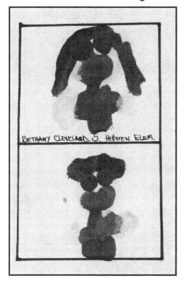

Samantha Wick Age 5
Hillview Elementary

Frankie Calire Age 6 St. Margaret's

Katherine Curry　Grade 2　Age 7　St. Mark

Steven Syracuse　Age 5　St. Margaret's

72

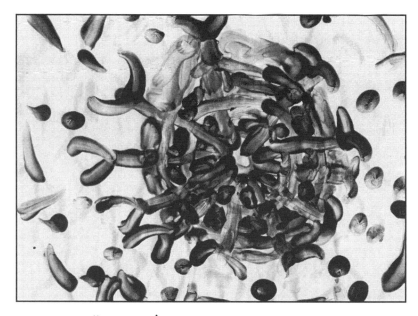

Sally O'Rourke   Grade 2   Age 7   St. Mark

Andrew Keysor   Grade 2   Age 7   St. Mark

73

Michelle Meer Age 6 St.Rose of Lima

Timmy Mahoney Age 6 St.Rose of Lima

Bill Webster Age 6 St. Margaret's

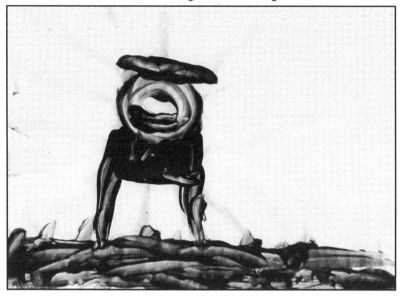

Brian O'connell Age 6 St. Mark

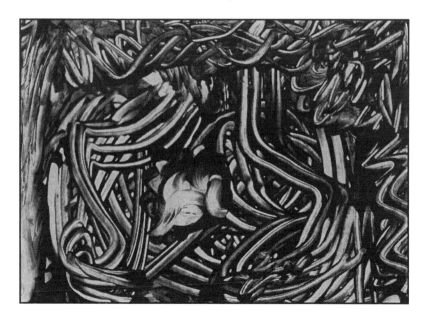

Amanda Rose Bernardi Age 9

Zack Lee Age 7
St.Peter and Paul

Cadie Dix Age 7
St.Peter and Paul

Little Michael's
Paper Jet

☆ ☆

This is the plane me and all my friends make because it's so easy. Even Gary's 4 year old brother Joey can make it. But we help him a little.

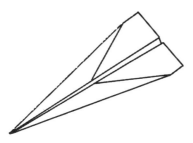

1. Here's how you make it. Cut out the whole page with scissors. Then cut out the rectangle on page 78.
2. Fold it in half on line A then open it again.
3. Fold both corners B to line A.
4. Keep them folded, then fold lines A-C in to the center.

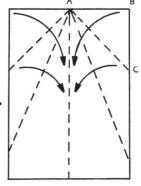

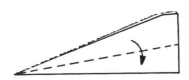

Fold the plane in half toward you and fold out the wings along the line.

Tips: If you want to try a loop, bend the wing tips up a little before you throw your really neat homemade plane. If you don't want to mess up your book you can make your plane out of an 8.5 x 11 sheet of paper.

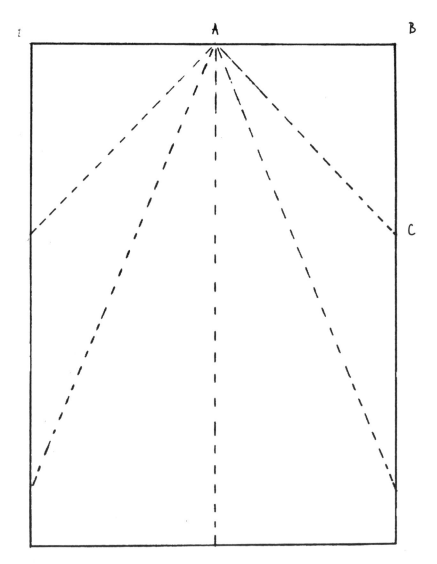

Little Michael's
☆ Paper Jet ☆
SECRET PLANS

33. So you remember

1. You were a kid

2. I'm curious

3. I'm not dad

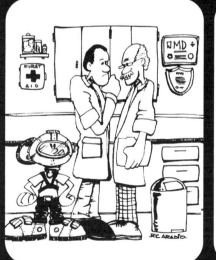

4. Stop yelling at me

5. I want some rules

6. Look at me

7. You shouldn't lie

8. TV isn't the same as you

9. I know all about sex

10. Take a vacation

11. I'm only seven

12. Because I said so

13. Let me make some mistakes

14. I could use some help

15. Stop promising

16. Don't argue when I'm home

17. I notice

18. I do what you do

19. Say you're Sorry

20. I'm only a kid once

21. I finally did it

22. You can't hug me too much

23. I want to be like Zeek

24. I really want you

84

25. Everyone needs love

Certificate of Accomplishment

This award goes to

_____ for reading

Little Michael's Guide to Raising Good Parents.

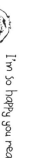

I'm so happy you read my book. I hope you get along better with your
kids now. And I'm really proud of you for caring so much.
I think your kids should take you for ice cream.

Love,
Little Michael

P.S. You can even get a banana split if you want!

Lessons From My Parents I've Carried Into Adulthood

"I haven't taught people in 50 years what my father taught by example in one week."

Mario Cuomo-Former Governor of New York

Someday Michael, your young friends might offer you alcohol and cigarettes, and you'll have to decide whether to accept them or not. I had one cigarette in 1980 and drink socially today. My father rarely told me what to do; he'd simply make suggestions and let me decide.

A childhood friend of mine used to perspire a lot. My father asked him in a matter of fact manner if he knew what body odor was. Then he calmly informed him he had it and suggested he try deodorant. He said it with a perfectly straight face. My father truly cared about helping him avoid embarrassment later in life.

When I was thirteen or fourteen my mom said to me: "Anything you do in life Michael, you choose to do." Those simple words taught me I was responsible for all my actions and also how I responded to the actions of others. Today, through writing and speaking I teach others ways of developing personal responsibility.

I was leading the Erie County Parks Department junior golf tournament. There were six holes left and I was playing well. My father unexpectedly showed up to watch me, and my game started to come apart. I blew the tournament and finished second by bogeying all six holes as he watched. Even though I was displeased with losing first place, having him take time to watch me was more important than winning. Today, it is still one of my fondest memories.

We were at B-Kwik supermarket in 1975 and had purchased a case (24 cans) of Blue Boy soda. As we exited through the automatic doors, dad realized we'd only been charged for six cans. So, we returned and informed the young checkout girl of the error and paid the correct amount. Today is July 21st, 1998 and ironically, I was accidentally undercharged by $4.50 at lunch. You can guess the rest of the story. Dad's lesson in honesty was never forgotten.

My brothers Frank and Chuck and I had healthy appetites back in grammar school. Mom would go through an entire loaf of Stroemann's bread making the three of us french toast or turn out twenty or thirty blueberry pancakes. She never stopped feeding us until we had our fill. Selflessness is something she possessed. We were too young to appreciate it at the time, but understand it's great value today.

My father owned Stenographic Institute of Western New York, which he founded. It was the first class of the year for would be stenographers. I was sitting in and observing, for the experience of it. Without a lot of fanfare, he warmly greeted the students then said, "I'd like you to know one thing before we start: four out of five of you won't be here after three months because you won't be willing to practice the three hours per night it requires to keep up." Brutal honesty, I later discovered, is usually far more beneficial than it may seem at the time.

My father always liked Cadillacs. However, he never bought a new one. He felt it was a waste of money, since cars depreciated so quickly. He was particularly proud of our 1973 royal blue coupe de ville. I was day dreaming about an earlier round of golf as I was driving home one day. I crossed the double yellow lines and hit another car head on, totalling both cars. The other driver and I both walked away from the accident unharmed. When I nervously called dad to break the news, his first words were, "Are you all right?" He never really got upset; I was amazed. Maturity had taught him that cars could be replaced, but loved ones could not.

My mother was valedictorian of her senior class. She had the highest four year average of everyone. She started out teaching math after graduation. However, once my parents started having children she chose to be a full time mother. There is not a more difficult or more important job on the planet. My siblings Lynn, Frank, Marie, Chuck, Stephanie, Christian, and I are all grateful she was there to raise us. We're eternally indebted.

My father had an unexpected heart attack in 1980 and was in the critical care unit at Sisters Hospital. I was sitting alone with him. Lying on his back, he was in a state I had never seen before, inactivity. He was always on the go, yet never appeared rushed to me. As I sat by his bedside, he tearfully spoke, apolgizing for not spending much time with me in the past. He said words I remember hearing only once from him: "I love you." It was also the first and last time we wept together. Those few minutes when we embraced were enough to last a lifetime. It's never too late to say those simple words, "I love you." If you haven't said them recently, go find your son or daughter, wrap your arms around them, and tell them.

Dad died on September 5th, 1980 at the age of forty-four. I've met hundreds of people from all walks of life who knew him. I never heard a bad word about him, while he was alive or since he died. There is no greater undertaking for me than to one day be thought of as my father was.

I had decided to attend Flagler college in St. Augustine, Florida. My dad passed away shortly before I was to leave Buffalo. I asked my mom if she wanted me to stay in Buffalo to help out. She said I should hold to my plans. She was forty-four with seven children between the ages of seven and twenty-one. Mom was proof we can survive even the most difficult situations.

Michael
Age 37

Excerpts from Parent's Little Book of Wisdom

by Buck Tilton and Melissa Gray

No one said it would be easy being a parent.

You will enjoy least in your child those things you enjoy least in yourself.

You are defined by your actions, not your words.

Do not expect love from a child who receives none.

Curiosity killed the cat. Your child is a human.

If there's any doubt about whether or not you should criticize your child, don't.

At least once a year watch How the Grinch Stole Christmas and The Lorax together. Make it a family tradition.

Take time to talk with your child's teachers.

Reprinted from Parent's Little Book of Wisdom © 1998 by Buck Tilton with permission from The Globe Pequot Press, Old Saybrook, CT, 1-800-243-0495, www.globe-pequot.com

Do not rush a child into growing up. There's no advantage
to being an adult.

What you put into loving your child is what you will get out.

Self-sacrifice is not a virtue. You will not help your children
by failing to take care of yourself.

No matter how expensive the toys you buy, he'll spend
more time banging rocks around inside a tin can.

Nothing in life is permanent.

Watch sunsets.

If you have taught them how to get along without you, you
have prepared them for life.

Please turn this page for an excerpt
from Michael Joseph Riso's
upcoming book

Little Michael
A Child's Wisdom
helping adults grow

A Continuous Learning Publishers book
available in November 1999

1. Exercise Is Fun

I go to school in the morning. I have to be there at 8:00. When I get there I can't wait until 9:45 because that's when gym starts. Sometimes we get to run real fast and see who is fastest. Once I was fastest of all. Running is so much fun I can't stand it. I can't wait to run again. Sometimes I try to run all the way home from the bus stop. Most all my friends like running and playing too.

I hear grown ups say they need to exercise, but I don't see them doing any. Maybe eating a lot of chips and cookies gives them enough exercise so they can feel good. But if eating helps how come they all look fat.

Hey, I can help! Come to my gym class at school. I'll show you how to run real fast. Then you can weigh 67 pounds like me!

2. Who Did It Anyway

I'm a good kid most always. My aunt and teachers, and mom and dad tell me so. I feel happy after I was good. I helped my grandma get out of her car last week and she said I was a wonderful girl. I feel glad when I hear nice things after I help other people. I'm not always that good. Sometimes I do something bad and get yelled at. I know when I did something wrong. Sometimes I feel very sad and cry.

I see grown ups do nice things for people. Then someone tells them how nice they were and they don't like it. I wonder why they don't feel good about being so nice. Other times they're not so nice. And someone tells them they were wrong and they talk like they didn't know better. I think they know. How come they pretend like someone else did it. Even I know what things I did. They should too.

3. You Can't Know It All

I just started riding my new bike. It has training wheels on it so I don't fall. They helped me because I was learning. Then my dad took them off and I could ride without a lot of help from my dad.

Mom gets mad when she falls going rollerblading. I tell her it's okay. But she doesn't have to fall so much. I asked her why she didn't have training wheels on her rollerblades. She said rollerblades don't have training wheels. I told her she could borrow my bike because she needs them bad!

4. I'm Glad You Got Married

We came home after playing tag with our friends. Mom and dad were holding hands and hugging each other. They looked so happy together.

Other times I wake up and eat my Cheerios and I see a note under my dad's danish that my mom put out for him. I peeked at the note once and it said, "I love you Mark. Thanks for being a wonderful husband and father."

Sometimes I come home from school and I see pretty red roses that are from dad to mom. My mom and dad are really nice to me and my sister, and our friends. We love them. We're happy they got married.

Mission

Continuous Learning Publishers books are created to help simplify people's lives. Each of us is given natural abilities that vary person to person. How we develop these abilities we're given at birth is up to each of us. As our lives become more complex it can at times be difficult to cope. We feel striving to enhance important areas of people's lives is a worthwhile undertaking. Our aim is to produce materials that make people's lives easier and more joyous.

About The Author

Michael Joseph Riso grew up in Buffalo, New York. After fourteen years in the golf business, he decided to write and speak full time. His message revolves around clarifying incorrect perceptions we all possess at times. Michael believes in the right of the individual to create, through one's own efforts, his or her life, as they would like it to be. He realizes too many of us use lack of formal schooling or a troubled upbringing as an excuse for where we are in life. If we can read, we can teach ourselves virtually anything, on almost any subject. If we can't read, we can learn that too. The answers are simple but not easy. Change yourself and your world will change.

Michael believes people can quickly right their unhappy lives by adhering to principles that have been proven over time. Our unhappiness, without exception, comes from denial of the way things are.

Michael's lecture topics include: "How To Live A Simple Centered Life" and "Becoming The Person Of Your Dreams." He can be contacted at Continuous Learning Publishers P. O. Box 162 Buffalo, NY 14231-0162, or by faxing 716-633-3254 or calling 716-633-0437.

About The Illustrator

I met RC Aradio through one of my friends and golf students, Rich Stilson. Little Michael's Guide To Raising Good Parents would be incomplete without RC's sketches and creative input. We produced this book as a team. From our first meeting to the actual printing of the book took under four months. RC taught me much about the benefits of listening when I was outside my area of expertise. He would let me ramble on when I felt certain about something I wanted, then say, "Let me show you something, quickly." When he was done, he had always created a masterpiece. Bob, thanks for creating Little Michael and letting him come to life through your wonderful sketches.

A Buffalo native, RC runs his design company, Targiin Studios, where his diverse talents allow him to create a vast range of artistic creations. His multi-faceted skills cover computer graphic design, oil painting, watercolors, sculpture, and photography. RC focuses his talents on fantasy, folklore, and cartooning which are captured in his premiere comic novel titled "The Targs". Some of his work can be seen at Lazer Park in Times Square, New York and at a children's playland sand sculpture at Riverside Park on West 83rd in Manhattan.

If you have an idea you would like to bring to life, you can contact RC through Continuous Learning Publishers by calling 716-633-0437.

Behind the scenes

The Making of a Dream

The Creative Team

• Little Michael • RC • Big Mike •

• STAGE 1 • THE SKETCH

• STAGE 2 • THE PENCIL

• STAGE 3 • THE INK

• THE TOY •

Did you Know there were:

• Over 30 separate revisions on the book's cover.

• Over 800 man hours spent writing, sketching, compiling, editing, inputting, and producing the finished book.

• 25 people critiquing the book before the final printing.

• 30 meetings between the author and illustrator within a 70 day period.

• 450 megabites of files & Storage.

Recipe

For a Successful Book

Bob and Mike's Home Brew

1 Complete Guide to Self Publishing* by Marilyn and Tom Ross
*would have been absolutely lost without it!
2 minds with limitless vision
2 parts chemistry
2 parts determination
Unparalleled respect for each other
Bob's incredibly understanding wife Jenni
Bob's naturally innocent child Kayla Mariin who kept us laughing
Many late night pizzas
2 bags ginger snaps
Numerous cups of tea and coffee
1 bag animal crackers
1 bag Oreo cookies
Bob's homemade sauce (best Mike's ever had-sorry grandma!)
2 minds influenced by Zen philosophy
Creative powers melding together
1 box freeze pops
Countless friends with honest critiques of the book before printing
1 bag Starburst
2 bowls of hard candy
1 bag M&M's
Bob's studio complete with 2 souped up Power Macintosh design
stations with ram and room to spare, 1 work horse color printer,
1 highly reliable scanner, 1 jazz, 1 zip, 1 fax modem, add photo
shop, stir in quark, plus a pinch of illustrator and 1 CD burner
The Star Wars trilogy
10 years of discipline
Overall support of our family and friends

Afterword

Little Michael is a character created out of the simplicity of a child's mind. My attempt was to communicate through eyes that were untarnished by much of today's societal pressure, pressure that beckons us to keep adding more to our lives instead of simplifying. The core of what is important to most of us-family, friends, loves, truth, and belief in a higher power should never be overlooked in exchange for attainment of the superficial.

We all learn through various methods of communication. Some learn most effectively by reading, others by looking at pictures or drawings, others by listening to the spoken word. Most people learn best by some combination of the three.

It is my sincere hope that some portion of Little Michael's attempt at simple communication has a positive influence on you or someone whom you care deeply about.

Michael Joseph Riso

Sources of help

Alcohol abuse
Alcoholics Anonymous-check your local yellow pages

Physical abuse
National Coalition Against Domestic Violence
1-800-799-SAFE

Drug abuse
The American Council For Drug Education
1-800-9HEROIN
1-888-MARIJUANA

Help for children
Kidspeace National Centers For Kids In Crisis
1-800-854-3123

Pregnancy
Planned Parenthood Federation of America-check your local yellow pages

Divorce, suicide, drugs, alcohol, physical/emotional abuse
Catholic Charities USA-check your local yellow pages

Education
Literacy Volunteers of America-check your local yellow pages

Sexual abuse
Rape, Abuse, & Incest National Network
1-800-656-HOPE

Emotional abuse/coping
APA Helpline
1-800-964-2000

Recommended Reading

Children Learn What They Live — Dorothy Law Nolte

Raising a Happy Confident Successful Child — Trish Magee

How to Behave So Your Children Will Too — Sal Severe Ph.D.

The One Minute Mother — Spencer Johnson M.D.

The One Minute Father — Spencer Johnson M.D.

Simplify Your Life With Kids — Elaine St. James

Questions Children Ask And How To Answer Them — Dr. Miriam Stoppard

Parent's Little Book Of Wisdom — Tilton/Gray

The Twelfth Angel — Og Mandino

A Better Way To Live — Og Mandino

The Little Engine That Could — Watty Piper

One Minute For Myself — Spencer Johnson M.D.

The Christmas Box — Richard Paul Evans

Recommended Reading (Con'd)

What You Think Of Me Is None Of My Business	Terry Cole Whittaker
Life's Little Instruction Book-Vol. II	H. Jackson Brown Jr.
The Delany Sisters' Book Of Everyday Wisdom	Amy Hill Hearth
What We Know So Far-Wisdom Among Women	Beth Benatovich

Recommended Audios

Secrets For Success and Happiness	Og Mandino
How To Be A No Limit Person	Dr. Wayne Dyer
Lead The Field	Earl Nightingale
The Strangest Secret	Earl Nightingale

Little Michael's Guide To
Raising Good Parents

MICHAEL JOSEPH RISO

Need additional copies for your:

- Son
- Daughter
- Brother
- Sister
- Wife
- Husband
- Grandmother
- Grandfather
- Mother
- Father
- In-law
- Friend

Order Form

Yes! Send me ___ copies of Litttle Michael's Guide To Raising Good Parents.

Name _____

Company _____

Address _____

City/state/zip _____

_____

Phone ( ) _____

Fax ( ) _____

Send me___copies $9.95 _____

S&H ($2 / book) _____

Subtotal _____

NY sales tax add 8% _____

Total Thank you! _____

Please send autographed gift copies _____

To: _____

_____

_____

From: _____

_____

_____

To: _____

_____

_____

From: _____

_____

_____

___check or money order (US) payable
   to: Continuous Learning Publishers

___charge my credit card

___Visa   ___MC   ___Discover

**All books will be signed: Michael Joseph Riso unless specified.

Card#_____ Exp.____

Signature_____

Credit card orders are toll free 24 hours a day.
Call 1-800-529-7960
You may Fax orders to us at 716-633-3254
Mail orders to: Continuous Learning Publishers
P.O. Box 162, Buffalo, NY 14231-0162
NO RISK ONE YEAR MONEY BACK GUARANTEE!